National Recognition of the Traditional Cultural Significance of X'unáxi (Indian Point)

Sealaska Heritage Institute is a private nonprofit founded in 1980 to perpetuate and enhance Tlingit, Haida, and Tsimshian cultures of Southeast Alaska. Its goal is to promote cultural diversity and cross-cultural understanding through public services and events. SHI also conducts social scientific and public policy research that promotes Alaska Native arts, cultures, history, and education statewide. The institute is governed by a Board of Trustees and guided by a Council of Traditional Scholars, a Native Artist Committee, and a Southeast Regional Language Committee.

SHI's **Box of Knowledge Series** consists of essays, reports, and books that the institute considers should be made available as a contribution to studies on Tlingit, Haida, and Tsimshian cultures, history, and languages. They may be based on work carried out by researchers working in collaboration with SHI, contributions prepared by external experts, and work by staff. Publications in the Box of Knowledge Series are available through SHI's website at www.sealaskaheritage.org.

Cover photo: View of Indian Point, Indian Island, and Pillar Rock. Courtesy of Beverly Demientieff.

Box of Knowledge graphic by Yukie Adams.
Book cover and layout by Brittany Gene.

SEALASKA HERITAGE INSTITUTE
105 S. Seward St., Suite 201
Juneau, Alaska 99801

978-1-946019-68-4

National Recognition of the Traditional Cultural Significance of X'unáxi (Indian Point)

By
Rosita K̲aaháni Worl, Ph.D.,
Thomas F. Thornton, Ph.D., &
Charles W. Smythe, Ph.D.

BOX OF KNOWLEDGE SERIES
SEALASKA HERITAGE INSTITUTE

Contents

Editor's Note

In 2009, the George Wright Society devoted a special issue of their journal *The George Wright Forum* to traditional cultural properties, which are historic properties eligible for listing in the National Register of Historic Places based on their traditional cultural significance. As guest editor of the issue, Dr. Chuck Smythe decided to feature X'unáxi as an excellent case study illustrating the dimensions of traditional cultural significance in accordance with National Register criteria. Due to the cultural and historical significance of X'unáxi, or Indian Point, near Auke Bay, Alaska, two of the papers have been republished in Sealaska Heritage's Box of Knowledge Series with permission from the George Wright Society.

The original traditional cultural property investigation of the Tlingit cultural landscape at X'unáxi was carried out by Thomas F. Thornton in 1996, amid concerns that planned development of Indian Point would threaten important Tlingit cultural sites there. Following Thornton's findings, the landowner (in this case the National Oceanic and Atmospheric Agency, or NOAA) made a determination that Indian Point was eligible for listing on the National Register for its traditional cultural significance. Sealaska Heritage Institute (SHI) prepared a nomination to the National Register a short time later, but other priorities prevented SHI from responding fully to review comments and completing the process until 2016 when X'unáxi was found eligible and listed in the National Register. The nomination had the support of Glacier Bay National Historical Park (National Park Service), Bureau of Land Management, Central Council of Tlingit and Haida Indian Tribes of Alaska, Douglas Indian Association, City and Borough of Juneau, and the concurrence from the Alaska State Historical Preservation Office.

Indian Point Not for Sale;
Or, Reflections on Indian Point

Rosita K̲aaháni Worl, Ph.D.

In the 1960s, I participated in an Alaska Native Sisterhood (ANS) ceremony that announced to the Tlingit world that I was to assume my mother's role after her death. I hadn't thought my responsibilities would begin so soon. The protection of Indian Point was to be my first public challenge.

I had received my mother's *kook̲éínaa*, which is a ceremonial banner, worn by members of the ANS and Alaska Native Brotherhood (ANB). Shortly after my mother's death, the ANS held a ceremony in which her ANS hat and banner were transferred to me. I had been selected because I had been under her formal training since the age of 10. My mother was a demanding teacher who observed my every action, even to the point of ensuring that I stood, sat, and held my head in the proper Tlingit manner. Her teaching also involved bringing me to her meetings.

After I received her *kook̲éínaa*, I returned home and sat on the beach in the front of our house reflecting on her contributions to the Tlingit people. She had worked tirelessly to secure political and economic equity for our people on multiple fronts. She worked as a union organizer for the salmon cannery workers and attended a continuous round of political meetings. She challenged the openly discriminatory practices towards the Tlingit that were prevalent throughout the 1940s and 1950s. Through her work and noble deeds, she had given my brothers and sisters a great gift. I wondered to myself what would I leave behind for my children.

4

Figure 1 Áak'w Indians preparing herring oil, Indian Point, ca. 1895. Photo courtesy of the Alaska State Library (P87-0081 Winter and Pond Photograph Collection).

I had grown up knowing that Indian Point was a Tlingit sacred site. At the time, I don't think I understood what the term "sacred" meant. However, I knew that it was a significant site and special to the Tlingit People. I was quite aware that I didn't have formal ties to Indian Point. My family was always reminded that we were "Chilkats" or Tlingits from the Haines and Klukwan area. I recall a prominent Áak'w Elder, Cecilia Kunz, repeatedly telling us that we were not "Juneau people" or Áak'ws, and that Juneau belonged to them. However, the Áak'w people were gracious in allowing us to use their land for subsistence hunting, fishing, and gathering. One of our favorite activities was gathering herring eggs at Indian Point (Figure 1).

Indian Point is significant to the Tlingit community. It is important to the Tlingit of the past, the Tlingit of the present, and the Tlingit of the future. It is a place where Tlingit people worked, played, laughed, and sang. It is a place where the Áak'w greeted their visiting neighbors. It is a place where our warriors and shamans conducted their purification and spiritual rites. It is a place that contains healing medicinal plants and powers. It is a place where our brothers and sisters, the raven and eagle, abound. It is a place where we buried our dead. It is a place where some day soon the Áak'w may re-inter the remains of ancestors who were taken away in the name of science and now may be reclaimed under the Native American Graves Protection and Repatriation Act. It is the place where the spirits of the ancestors of the Áak'w Kwáan inhabit. It is a place where we sing our songs to our ancestors and call for spiritual assistance. It once was an important subsistence area until it was polluted after the non-Tlingit began to develop the northern shores of Indian Point. It is also a place that is highly coveted by others, but Indian Point is a sacred site to the Tlingit.

While we may dress as white people and speak the language of the white man, our hearts remain true to our old ways. Tlingit people have been reluctant to speak openly about our beliefs and our spiritual relationships to our ancestors lest they unleash the wrath of the proselytizing agents who sought to eradicate Native spiritual beliefs. We, who grew up during a period when Tlingit culture was repressed and were punished for speaking our language, are hesitant to openly discuss our beliefs lest we subject ourselves and our children to ridicule. However, we came to realize that we had to explain our spiritual beliefs so that non-Natives would understand our opposition to the construction of a governmental facility at Indian Point.

Tlingit people are culturally different from the larger society not simply because we have different cultural beliefs and practices. We conceive of space, time, life, and death in a different way than non-Tlingit.

Indian Point is a burial site, but it is unlike a Western cemetery. As I understand it, when Westerners and those who adhere to their beliefs bury their dead, they believe that their souls go to a place called heaven or hell. They do not seem to mind if their graves have to be moved

6

Figure 2 View of Indian Point and Indian Island from Auke Bay. Photo by Rico Worl.

to make way for progress and development. I respect the rights of those who espouse such beliefs, but they are unlike traditional Tlingit ideologies.

Traditional Tlingit people believe that when we die, our spiritual being divides, with one part going to a supernatural abode and the other remaining at the site where our physical remains are interred. We respect the burial grounds inhabited by the spirits of our ancestors. Sacred grounds, such as Indian Point, bond us to the land, they unite us with our ancestors, they unify us with our living Tlingit brethren, and they ensure our survival as Tlingit people through future generations. The spirits of shamans remain powerful even after their death and can also bring both harm and good will and fortune depending on whom and the manner in which his or her spirit is approached. Burial sites embody the Tlingit cycle of life–death–life. Even to this day as I fly into Juneau and pass Indian Point, I call for spiritual assistance, and I reach to my heart to throw out any illnesses I may have. This site is sacred to the Áak'w Ḵwáan. Indian Point is sacred to the Tlingit.

We Tlingit who are from other areas outside of Juneau acknowledge the aboriginal tie of the Áak'w to Juneau and Indian Point irrespective of the fact that the Áak'w no longer hold legal title to the land. We stood unified with the Áak'w people because of this recognition and because we share the same beliefs and concerns. We knew that if the desecration and destruction of this sacred site can occur, they will occur elsewhere.

Shortly after receiving my mother's *kookéinaa*, I learned that the city of Juneau intended to rezone and subdivide Indian Point and to sell residential lots. The Native community was extremely upset. We all knew the significance of Indian Point. I called my fellow brothers and sisters from ANB and ANS to testify at the city council meeting in opposition to the proposed action. [Editor's note: for a discussion of this meeting, including Worl's testimony, see Tom Thornton's paper in this volume.] I was joined by several other Tlingit people. I thought we should have a greater representation, and I ran out of the meeting onto the street and asked those Tlingit people whom I saw to join us and to testify against the action. I also called my friend Tommy Richards, who was a reporter with the *Tundra Times*, the statewide Native newspaper, to help us by bringing attention to our plight.

We were successful in persuading the city council of the importance of Indian Point to the Tlingit, and they tabled their action to sell the residential lots. In retrospect, I can see that we were quite naïve in thinking that Indian Point would be forever protected.

In the summer of 1996, when I assumed the position of interim president of the Sealaska Heritage Foundation (now renamed the Sealaska Heritage Institute, or SHI), I was startled to find, amidst the mounds of paper left on my desk by my predecessor, a letter to a former SHI president about the draft report on historic and prehistoric heritage associated with a proposed development of Indian Point. Nearly 30 years after my first episode with Indian Point, the federal government proposed to build an office complex and research center there. I immediately held a meeting with our SHI board of trustees. I briefed them on the proposed action and one trustee, who was also a clan leader, told me in no uncertain terms that we would die to protect the burial sites of our shamans. I quickly responded to the author of the letter (and the study) and noted that the legally required "consultation" with the Native community had not occurred. I instantly wrote a letter to that effect to the agency and asked for the status of the project. The Native community quickly responded, expressing opposition to the facility and insisting on formal consultations.

An archaeologist who had been under contract to assess Indian Point visited me. He advised me that he had met and consulted with a number of Tlingit elders to discuss the project. I reminded him that discussions with individual elders did not constitute consultation.

A few months after this discussion, the responsible federal agency, the National Oceanic and Atmospheric Administration (NOAA), organized a series of meetings with me and with the community. One meeting in particular stands out in my memory. We met in the Centennial Hall, and a number of Tlingit people testified to the agency representatives about the importance of Indian Point. We cried as a young Tlingit woman and man tried to hold back their tears as they spoke about the significance of Indian Point and their concern about the potential desecration of the site. The young man, who was from Angoon (a nearby Native village), told of burning food there to transfer the food to his deceased relatives.

During one of these meetings, I noted the non-compliance with Section 106 consultation, and that the cultural resource study did not assess the site as a traditional cultural property (TCP) and did not investigate the dynamic relationship between the tangible and intangible cultural resources and the Tlingit beliefs and practices and values associated with Indian Point. I also said that Native people would pursue all administrative and legal options for the protection of Indian Point, which could delay the project. We also asked NOAA to consider the other two sites that had been identified in the Juneau area as possible sites for the facility. We understood that some within their ranks viewed one of the sites as acceptable.

One of the federal agency officials asked me what could be done to "mitigate the adverse impacts." I recall thinking to myself for a moment, and then offered that I didn't know if spirits could be contained to a specific area if a fence were to be constructed to keep the spirit enclosed and the public away. I also emphasized that our sacred sites were unlike those of non-Natives, which could be deconsecrated, such as a church that is transformed into a meeting hall. I told them, however, that I would think about their question.

I recommended that a TCP evaluation be conducted. I had recently attended a Keepers of the Treasures meeting sponsored by the National Park Service in the Southwest and learned about TCPs. I thought that Indian Point was a perfect candidate for a TCP. I suggested that they contract with a Native entity.

Although I am an anthropologist and was thoroughly familiar with the history of Indian Point, I knew full well that the government would not ask me to conduct the study. I suggested a number of possible anthropologists who were familiar with the Tlingit culture. To do the study, a colleague at the University of Alaska was contracted (see Tom Thornton's paper in this volume). Additionally, NOAA also contracted with a traditional Tlingit leader to meet with the Áak'w people. I interpreted this effort as a measure to divide the Tlingit community.

In early 1997, before the TCP study was started, I learned that NOAA was offering us $1 million and 50 acres of land in the Auke Village Recreation Area if we would drop our opposition to the construction project at Indian Point. They suggested that we could use the funds to build a village at another site. We were indignant with the offer. At the same time, we sadly recognized that some of our people might not hold Indian Point in the same regard as we did, and could well be tempted by the million-dollar offer. The powerful governmental entity wanted the Áak'w and the Tlingit to redefine and restructure their culture and ideologies to meet its need. The clan mother of the Áak'w, Rosa Miller, adamantly opposed the destruction and desecration of their sacred site. She did not believe that the sanctity and spiritual attributes of Indian Point could be transferred to another site to satisfy the federal agency. The Áak'w immediately rejected the offer.

The Tlingit community stood solidly behind their decision. The Native community, including the Áak'w Ḵwáan, Douglas Indian Association, ANB, ANS, Central Council of Tlingit and Haida Indian Tribes of Alaska, Sealaska Corporation, and SHI opposed the construction of a building at Indian Point. However, one Tlingit individual, who had lived away from home for decades, urged her fellow Áak'w to accept the offer and warned that they would probably lose anyway, and the powerful government would eventually build on the sacred site. The clan mother knew that if her people accepted the money, they stood to lose intangible treasures of their heritage that no amount of money could buy—least of all their honor. This clan mother, who was trained through her lifetime in the ways of her ancestors, stood her ground against the federal government.

At one point, I was called into the office of the chief executive officer (CEO) of Sealaska Corporation. Sealaska Corporation is the regional Native corporation established under the Alaska Native Claims Settlement Act (ANCSA) of 1971, which resolved our aboriginal land claims with the government. After its formation, Sealaska Corporation created an affiliate organization, SHI, whose mission was to protect and perpetuate the Tlingit, Haida, and Tsimshian cultures of Southeast Alaska. The CEO advised me that the powerful senior US senator of Alaska, Ted Stevens, had called him and asked why the Tlingit were opposing the construction of the NOAA facility. The senator conveyed that he was trying to help the economy of Juneau. Our CEO responded that when it came to cultural matters, he was required to yield to the traditional leaders and elders. I also reminded our CEO that very few of our tribal members had jobs with NOAA. I was also to learn later that the new facility would be named after our Senator Stevens.

Those who supported the construction of the NOAA facility at Indian Point blamed the Native community for the delay of the construction project. They claimed that we would be responsible if the funds for the NOAA facility were lost. From my perspective, the delay in construction could not be attributed to the Native community. Had NOAA met the federal requirements of consultation, they would have learned that Indian Point is a sacred site. They would have known that the Tlingit community would oppose the development on these grounds, and perhaps they would have known that they should have selected an alternative site for their facility.

I was at a loss to understand why it was expected that Indians must allow one of their sacred sites to be put in jeopardy and to sacrifice our beliefs because a governmental entity wanted to build an office facility on our sacred lands. I was exasperated that the federal employees rejected another possible site for the facility as "not acceptable" because the 45-minute drive was too far for them to commute.

At this point in my life, I was somewhat more knowledgeable of the laws that might offer us some protections. However, I also fully understood that we could go through the required legal process and ultimately, a decision could be made that was adverse to our Tlingit interests. I met privately with the NOAA officials and conveyed to them that we would use all the resources available to us to halt and delay the construction of the facility at Indian Point, even if it meant going to court. We recognized that we could lose Indian Point to a powerful government agency; however, we were determined, as our trustees had directed, "to die to protect a shaman's burial site."

The Áak'w have lost all of their traditional territory to those of us who have moved into Juneau. Today all of us enjoy the beauty and bounty of this land. We felt that it was imperative that the Áak'w and the Tlingit people be allowed to maintain this sacred site.

In 2002, we nominated Indian Point for inclusion in the National Register and submitted the nomination to the Alaska State Historic

Preservation Office for concurrence. In the subsequent months and years, we continued to respond to the seemingly unending questions posed by the office. I attended a Historical Commission meeting in Anchorage to request the status of our nomination and was advised that approval was imminent. However, when I attended a follow-up meeting in Juneau in 2006, we were again asked for additional information, which again we provided. We have since contacted the office several times asking about the status of the nomination. The federal agency, NOAA, determined Indian Point to be eligible as a TCP for inclusion in the National Register of Historic Places in 1997. However, we continue to await the State Historic Preservation Office's decision. For many years, Native people have had a strained relationship with the state of Alaska over the protection of our subsistence rights under federal law. Early this year, I wrote yet another letter to the State Historic Preservation Office asking for its decision.

This experience prompted us to add the selection of sacred sites to our legislative initiative. As a member of the board of directors of Sealaska Corporation, I reported to the board that we had been actively working on this TCP nomination for ten years (since 1997). I conveyed that we needed another mechanism to protect our historic and sacred sites in view of the time and energy we had expended to try to protect just *one* sacred site. I reported to the board that we were preparing to publish a cultural atlas which included over 3,000 place names in the Tlingit and Haida languages, and I felt that we had to do something different to protect our sacred sites. I also proposed that we look at the possibility of creating a Tongass Heritage Area in Southeast Alaska. At this time, we were working to finalize Sealaska Corporation's land entitlement in Congress to ensure the conveyance of all lands due to us, which would require an amendment to ANCSA. The board of directors decided that we would include in the proposed legislation 4,000 acres for sacred and historic sites. Corporations do not generally own or seek the ownership of non-productive or non-economic lands. However, as a Native corporation, we view our cultural survival and the protection of our sacred sites as major objectives along with our financial enterprises. At this time, we have introduced legislation in Congress to amend ANCSA to allow us to select and maintain ownership of a significant number of our sacred sites. We also continue to advance the notion of heritage areas as another mechanism to protect our historical and sacred sites.

Indian Point offers a clear lesson that can be learned or affirmed: that we as Native Americans view the protection of our sacred sites as essential, and we will avail ourselves of every mechanism to do so. We are not apologetic that our cultural beliefs may conflict with Western values or stand in the way of progress or the construction of a new facility. Our cultural values must be interpreted and applied on their own merit and not defined or structured in the context of national laws or needs.

Rosita Kaaháni Worl, Ph.D., is Tlingit of the Shangukeidí clan and the House Lowered from the Sun in Klukwan, Alaska. Worl, an anthropologist, serves as president of the Sealaska Heritage Institute.

Anatomy of a Traditional Cultural Property: The Saga of Auke Cape

Thomas F. Thornton, Ph.D.

In an era when Indigenous people face limited sovereignty, minority status, and continuing pressure on traditional lands and resources, how can important cultural landscapes best be conserved as living landscapes? For Native Americans, the process for evaluating and conserving traditional cultural properties (TCPs), first introduced twenty years ago, constituted a small but important governmental response to the accelerating problem of erosion of their communal lands and historical and sacred sites. National Register Bulletin 38 offered a set of guidelines for evaluating these places as "living landscapes" of national historical significance due to their association with "cultural practices or beliefs of a living community that (a) are rooted in the community's history, and (b) are important in maintaining the continuing cultural identity of a community." If a cultural property receives a positive evaluation, it can then be nominated for inclusion in the National Register of Historic Places. To mitigate a property's vulnerability in the interim between a positive eligibility determination and the completion of the nomination process, the property can be treated "as if" it had been successfully nominated and placed on the Register by the keeper. This procedure is followed because often agencies do not have the time and resources necessary to complete the formal nomination process; the interim listing provides protection until the formal nomination process is completed.

Traditionally, the Register had been biased toward non-Native landscapes of significance—battlefields, architectural marvels, pioneer

16

trails, etc.—based primarily on the antiquity of material remains
and a rather singular interpretive framework for how these sites fit
into the master narrative of the nation's or region's development and
character. Although sites on the Register can be of local, regional, or
national significance, the bias was nearly always toward the physical
and material objectification of history in a "built" environment (i.e.,
structures, landscapes, etc.). This framework held little regard for places
of continuing symbolic and material significance to Native American
communities, and so they remained either unprotected or invisible,
or both. Hence, there was a need for new guidelines to address these
kinds of cultural properties.

There is no question that the TCP process and criteria are more
inclusive than those of the conventional Register, but the critical
political–ecological questions remain: what is being conserved and
for whom under the guise of historic sites conservation in the United
States? Has the TCP process helped conserve cultural landscapes
of significance to Native American communities? In Alaska, where
not a single Alaska Native TCP has been formally recommended for
inclusion in the National Register by the State Historic Preservation
Office, despite positive eligibility determinations and nominations,
the answer is unequivocally "not yet." To understand why not yet, it is
useful to examine the saga of Auke Cape (also known as Indian Point),
a Tlingit TCP found eligible for inclusion, with concurrence from the
Alaska State Historic Preservation Office, and first nominated for the
Register more than a decade ago based on an investigation I conducted
in 1997 (Thornton 1997), but which continues to languish in the
Register "approval" process for a variety of reasons not altogether clear.

In this essay, I examine the Auke Cape TCP case as a means for
evaluating the efficacy of the TCP process itself. In doing so, I draw on
what I term a political ecology of cultural models framework. Political
ecology examines how humans compete for, manage, and impact
"scarce" environmental resources, such as land, trees, fish, and wildlife,
from a political-economy and ecological perspective. Cultural models
(cf. Holland and Quinn 1987; Shore 1998) theory posits that human

groups possess shared and distributed cognitive frames which play a critical role in coordinating their thoughts and actions in response to environmental phenomena, including landscapes such as Auke Cape. Combining the two theoretical strains, *a political ecology of cultural models* examines how differing cultural models of environmental phenomena compete—often unequally—in shaping collective perceptions and actions towards particular landscapes, including historic sites and traditional cultural properties.

Negotiating cultural models of Auke Cape in the 1960s

The dominant cultural model of Auke Cape, among non-Natives especially, is that of a prime waterfront landscape. The property defines one side of Auke Bay, the premier harbor in Alaska's capital city of Juneau and a favored settlement site for its access, views, sun, and shelter among the city's 30,000 residents. By the end of the 20th century, Auke Cape stood out as an oasis of undeveloped public land along the otherwise highly developed waterfront corridor between Juneau's downtown and greater Mendenhall Valley. The waterfront peninsula was divided into separate lots managed by the National Park Service (NPS), which developed a portion as employee housing and a dock serving Glacier Bay National Park, and the city and borough of Juneau. Pro-development forces in the city viewed the property as ripe for commercial development and a residential subdivision, while others saw it as an important habitat and scenic recreation area to be maintained in its present state. Efforts to develop the non-federal portion of the property for waterfront housing and other facilities in the late 1960s were defeated by a coalition of Native and non-Native groups seeking to protect the forested peninsula in its present condition. Though politically on the same side, the Natives and non-Natives argued from different cultural models of the landscape. Non-Natives stressed the peninsular landscape's beauty and pristine character and its potential for recreation. Natives, in contrast, primarily stressed the peninsula's significance as Áak'w K̲wáan (Áak'w Tlingits') *at.óow* (sacred property), including its status as a historic settlement, fort, subsistence, and burial site. These two cultural models coalesced into a successful united front against the cultural model of "development" for Auke Cape because, despite their different primary conceptualizations of the landscape, they were in consensus in opposing any significant alteration of the site's character.

The Juneau-based *Southeast Alaska Empire* newspaper reported on the pivotal testimony at a May 10, 1969, public hearing which helped convey Tlingit conceptualizations of the property to non-Natives and seal the defeat of efforts to rezone Auke Cape for residential development.

> Eight members of the Tlingit and Haida tribes spoke at the Wednesday Borough Assembly hearing to decide whether Indian Point should become a private residential area or be turned to public use
>
> Rosetta [Rosita] Rodriguez [now Worl, see her companion essay in this volume], Amos Wallace, Mrs. Edward [Cecilia] Kunz, Nellie Bennett, Hank Cropley, Mrs. Nora Florendo [now Dauenhauer], and Mrs. Anita Engeberg.
>
> Mrs. Rodriguez, who is Chairman of the A.N.B. Heritage Committee and Secretary of Tlingit and Haidas, said in a prepared statement:
>
> "Indian Point is more than an issue of land or a possible source of revenue. It represents to us a link to our past, our forefathers, and our way of life. Perhaps you may understand this feeling if you think of the many historical sites and monuments, such as Plymouth Rock where the pilgrims first landed, or Abraham Lincoln's humble one-room log cabin, or of the Statue of Liberty. The Federal government has seen fit to designate these and many other areas historical sites. Indian Point is all this to us. . . ."
>
> She concluded by expressing the hope that the Assembly would "see that Indian Point would better

serve its citizens by becoming an area where all may go to enjoy its natural grandeur, where Tlingits may continue in their traditional activities."

Others affirmed the historical nature of the sites because of Indians buried there and because of the herring spawn fishery conducted on the shore.

Without this cross-cultural appeal to non-Indigenous cultural models of landscape conservation, it is unlikely the Tlingit *at.óow* paradigm of historic preservation would have prevailed on its own in protecting Auke Cape, at least not beyond the burial sites. Tlingits were already a minority in Juneau and their "property rights" were theoretically being "settled" through separate federal claims process (consummating, ultimately, in the Alaska Native Claims Settlement Act of 1971). What is more, few material traces of their long historical presence on the land had been documented in the archaeological record, and there was no process in place for recognizing the multitude of material and non-material cultural associations with the land as a "link to our past, our forefathers, and our way of life," or what Tlingits term their *shagóon*, "heritage and destiny" (see de Laguna 1972; Dauenhauer and Dauenhauer 1987; Thornton 2008). The National Historic Preservation Act (NHPA) of 1966 itself was only a few years old. Thus, Tlingits had to argue by analogy (to non-Native monuments) and appeal to the dominant non-Native historical and recreational values in order to make their case for protecting their historic landscape. Such was the political ecology of cultural models in the late 1960s; Native models had little valence.

With this victory, the bulk of the 78-acre Auke Cape property remained undeveloped for the next three decades. However, the fate of the peninsula came to a head again in September 1996, when the National Oceanic and Atmospheric Administration (NOAA) selected Auke Cape as its preferred site for constructing a new consolidated office and research laboratory facility in Juneau. As they had 30 years previously, local and regional Native organizations opposed this alternative due to concerns for cultural and historic values associated with the site. By this time Auke Cape had become divided into four large lots (see Figure 1) controlled by several different entities. The two southern and outermost lots (Lots 3 and 4, which had been tagged for development in the 1960s) continued to be property of the city and borough of Juneau. Lot 1 at Indian Cove is federal land managed by the National Park Service as a support facility for Glacier Bay National Park. Lot 2, the largest undeveloped lot, was conveyed to NOAA by the Bureau of Land Management for potential development of the consolidated facility. However, part of this original lot, now known as Lot 2A, remained under the control of the Bureau of Land Management, and was not included in the transfer of land to NOAA because of evidence of Indian graves on the site. A recreational trail, maintained by the City and Borough of Juneau, the Park Service, and volunteers, wends its way through parts of all four lots before terminating at Indian Point on the end of the peninsula. Beyond this, the tidelands surrounding the cape are owned by the state of Alaska.

Through provisions set out in the Alaska Native Claims Settlement Act (ANCSA), Section 14(h)1, for protecting Native cemetery and historic sites, Juneau-area Natives, now organized into regional (Sealaska) and village (Goldbelt) corporations, identified Auke Cape as a historic settlement and grave site in their survey (Sealaska 1975:824). However the site was not thoroughly surveyed, in part due to the split federal–state jurisdiction (state lands could not be selected) and potentially competing allotment and other claims on the land. Undoubtedly, additional historic sites could have been confirmed had there been more time and resources available for assessment of sites. Without protection under 14(h)1 or other provisions, the bulk of Auke Cape remained open to development.

The 1996 TCP evaluation and nomination

Fortunately, by 1996, the process of assessing environmental and cultural impacts of development projects on federal lands had been significantly enhanced, thanks to the National Environmental Policy Act (NEPA; 1969) and the NHPA. Under Section 106 of NHPA, federal agencies were required to take into account the effect of their projects ("federal or federal-assisted undertakings") on sites that are included in or eligible for inclusion in the National Register of Historic Places. Amendments to NHPA in 1992 provided a greater

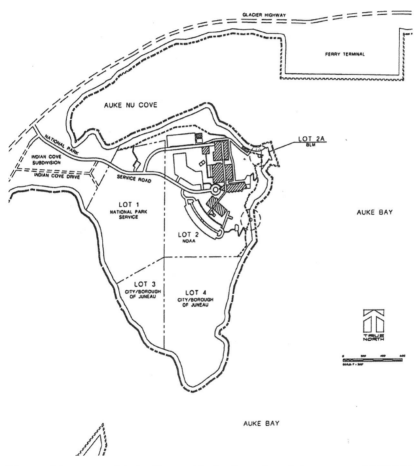

Figure 1 Lot map of Auke Cape with the footprint of the proposed NOAA/NMFS Consolidated Facility. The boundaries of the proposed TCP include Lots 1–4 and offshore islands (Indian Island, Pillar Rock). Source: NOAA 1998.

role for Indian tribes in federal and state preservation programs and added greater federal responsibility for the identification, evaluation, and nomination of historic properties to the National Register of Historic Places, and for consideration of historic properties during agency decision-making. The 1996 regulations provided greatly expanded guidance and requirements for consultation with Indian tribes in the process of taking into account the effects of the agency's undertaking on historic properties. This provision triggered the need for a cultural resource survey of Indian Point, the need to document and evaluate whether any properties might be eligible for inclusion in the National Register, and the need for consultation with Indian tribes in these efforts. In addition, Bulletin 38 had been issued in 1990, defining procedures for assessing and protecting TCPs, including landscapes with significant non-tangible attributes, such as religious beliefs and ancestral traditions.

With all of these changes, it seemed that the Tlingit *at.óow* model of sacred possession could be more fully recognized in the process of assessing NOAA's proposed facility. Indeed, the draft environmental impact statement (required under NEPA) on the consolidated facility noted up front that "the site's location, near Auke Bay, Auke Creek, and Auke Lake, and a short distance from the traditional winter Áak'w Village, makes it likely that Native resources are located on the site." Cultural resource surveys of the proposed building tract were conducted in 1992 and 1996 by Charles M. Mobley. Through archaeological surveying on the building site (Lot 2) and limited interviews and archival research, Mobley was able to develop a picture of past occupancy and land use of the area. Historic human activities and sites included salmon and herring egg fisheries; cockle, clam, and other marine invertebrate harvesting; some 31 culturally modified hemlock trees (modified, among other reasons, for the inner bark which is a prized Native food); four canoe runs; smokehouses; camping sites; and burial grounds. Mobley (1996:46–47) concluded that portions of the building tract, namely the canoe runs and the midden upslope from those runs (together given Alaska Heritage

Resources Survey number JUN-701) are eligible for the National Register of Historic Places based on criterion D, their potential to yield information important to our understanding of prehistory or history. Among his mitigation considerations, Mobley (1996:48) suggested that this area be avoided in development of the facility, as construction would "likely obliterate any cultural resources in its footprint." His conclusions bolstered the public testimony on the part of local Tlingits, and the initial findings of the 1975 Sealaska historic sites survey.

As a consequence, federal and Native leaders agreed that a TCP evaluation should be conducted on Auke Cape to determine if all or parts of the area might be eligible for nomination to the National Register of Historic Places. My TCP investigation was initiated in late April 1997. Between April and June 1997, I reviewed documentary and oral sources of information pertaining to Auke Cape and conducted more than 40 interviews with local Tlingits and others familiar with the history and uses of the property (Thornton 1997). Results of the investigation revealed that Áak'w Tlingits conceive of Auke Cape as a single property, that the boundaries of the site, called X'unáxi in Tlingit (referring to its earliest use as a stopover and camping place), encompass not only Auke Cape but the nearshore areas of Auke Nu Cove and Indian Cove and the immediate offshore islands (Indian Island and "Pillar Rock"; Figure 2), and that Áak'w Tlingits repeatedly have fought to maintain both the integrity of condition of Indian Point and their relationship and rights to the site in the face of increasing encroachments.

Further, the property was found to be historically significant in four major respects. First, the Indian Cove side of Auke Cape, also known as Fairhaven, is the original habitation site of the Áak'w Kwáan in the Juneau area. Members of the Yaxtetaan (Dipper House) of the L'eineidí (Dog Salmon) clan moved with their leader from Young Bay, ultimately landing at Auke Cape/Indian Cove (X'unáxi). Here the group erected the first Dipper House (matrilineal clan house) in Juneau and lived prosperously for some time; eventually, the village

Figure 2 Pillar Rock, part of the Indian Point/Auke Cape Traditional Cultural Property. Photo courtesy of the author.

was moved a short distance northward to what is now the site of Auke Recreation area where the name Anchgaltsoow ("Town that Moved") was applied to the new settlement. Second, X'unáxi was—until the decline of the herring run—a hallowed subsistence site for fishing and gathering activities. Third, Auke Cape and its nearshore islands are the site of historic Native graves, including shaman graves. Shaman graves constitute particularly powerful landscapes that extend some distance beyond the actual above-ground burial sites and generally are avoided out of respect for the power of the spirit(s) that continue to dwell in their midst. Fourth, Auke Cape is a historic lookout, refuge site, and meeting place for major events in Áak'w Ḵwáan history, including battles and encounters with other groups in which key Yaxtetaan leaders, in typical Northwest Coast Indian fashion, earned their prestigious titles and through which the clan established its preeminent status as owners of Auke Bay and the surrounding territory. Collectively, these characteristics defined Auke Cape as a cultural property of deep and abiding cultural significance, a critical component of the Áak'w Ḵwáan history, *at.óow*, and *shagóon*.

The report concluded that the cultural beliefs and practices associated with Auke Cape meet the guidelines established in National Register Bulletin 38 for evaluating Register-eligible traditional cultural properties. Auke Cape is *deeply rooted in the community's history*, and the tangible resources associated with the site *are important in maintaining the continuity and identity of the community*. The report also found that the site meets criteria for eligibility to the National Register because it is (a) associated with key events of the Áak'w Ḵwáan, (b) associated with key persons of significance, and (c) likely to yield more significant findings concerning the history and prehistory of Southeast Alaska. I found no obvious conditions that would make the property ineligible for the National Register. The landscape still held its integrity as a historic site, vital to the contemporary Áak'w Tlingit community. Similarly, the shamans' burial ground remained a potent influence on Tlingits from other communities, such as Hoonah, who observe the culturally prescribed avoidances and gestures of respect when passing the site when coming in and out of Auke Bay.

Federal officials were, at first, dubious about the cultural values of the property. In particular, they misunderstood the Tlingit model of claiming the property by revealing oral histories about how it came to be possessed as *at.óow*. One of these oral histories, the story of how Yeeskanaalx ("Newly Rich Man") got his name, was told by Áak'w Ḵwáan leader Rosa Miller at meeting concerning the proposed consolidated facility in 1997. Her mother, Bessie Visaya (Visaya 1972), Cecilia Kunz (Kunz 1997) and Forrest DeWitt (DeWitt 1985) also have recorded versions of this story, part of which is also recounted in John R. Swanton's well-known *Tlingit Myths and Texts* (1909:58ff). The basic details of the story are as follows:

At Auke Cape, an Áak'w Ḵwáan leader (Ḵuwudakaá) meets, challenges, and ultimately defeats a Yakutat

(Tlingit community to the north) rival in a display of wealth—thus earning the name Yeeskanaalx ("Newly Rich Man"). The conflict was precipitated by the Yakutat leader's failure to pay a visit to the Áak'w leader during a trip down to the Taku River. On the way back north from Taku River, a messenger was sent out to the point (Indian Point at the tip of Auke Cape, in most versions of the story) to invite the Yakutat group (the Loox'eidí clan) ashore at X'unáxi (Auke Cape) for a feast at which the Áak'w leader proceeded to insult the Yakutat leader by burning the decorated prow of his canoe in the fire.

Angry, the Yakutat chief left, but returned to X'unáxi the following spring to settle the score. A quarrel began and soon the Yakutat leader started throwing copper shields (*tináa*)—symbols of wealth—into the water to show his superior status. The Áak'w chief responded in kind by bringing out his own coppers and disposing of them in the water. The Áak'ws also brought forth a young woman who imitated her crest, the dog salmon, in a spawning dance, except that instead of laying eggs she deposited valuable things like copper bracelets and abalone into the water, another symbolic gesture to demonstrate the superior wealth and status of the Áak'w group. Soon the Yakutat leader ran out of coppers and his group resorted to substituting spruce bark. Although they weighted the spruce bark with rocks so it would sink like the coppers, somehow it re-floated and their ruse was exposed. Victorious, the Áak'ws then sang an insulting song, prompting the Yakutat group to give up in shame.

From this event, Kuwudakaa earned his new title, Yeeskanaalx ("Newly Rich Man"). The Loox'eidí, it is said, have never been seen since.

NOAA officials were baffled as to why Miller would tell this story, as the events themselves—involving conflict, rivalry, and deception—seemed, as one official put it to me privately, "pitiful." But in Tlingit cultural logic, it was a kind of "title search" to show how the Áak'w Ḵwáan had come to own Auke Cape legitimately, and had their claims to it as cultural property validated publicly. However, rather than culminating in a written legal document, the Tlingit model of property ownership concentrates on the *event* of title purchase, which becomes a constituent part of their own identity and status as a community, as embodied in the very names of their leaders, like Yeeskanaalx, as well as the story and the song, all of which are carried still today. In the Tlingit cultural model, the surrender and retreat of the Yakutat L'oox'eidí in the face of the Áak'w song is also important, for it established that the Áak'w claim was accepted by competing groups. The public performance and ritual validation of the story of Yeeskanaalx is thus the legal starting point for defending Auke Cape as Áak'w Ḵwáan cultural property.

Denouement or irresolution?

My report and positive findings concerning the eligibility of Auke Cape as a TCP were accepted by the lead federal agency, NOAA, and reported in the final environmental impact statement on the Auke Cape facility (NOAA 1998). The site was determined officially to be eligible for inclusion in the National Register of Historic Places as a TCP. As a result, an alternative site (Lena Point) was chosen for development of what would become the Ted Stevens Marine Research Institute, named for the state's influential US senator, who had helped originally to secure federal money to build the facility. Significantly, from a cultural models standpoint, in explaining the decision to move the facility from Auke Cape to Lena Point, Juneau's vice mayor did not explicitly recognize the value of Auke Cape as a Tlingit TCP worthy of protection, but simply stated that the site had "cultural problems." The new $51 million institute finally opened in the spring of 2007, and to this day Natives are blamed for the delay.

Meanwhile, the fate of Auke Cape as a cultural property has languished in the state's historic preservation bureaucracy. Shortly after the 1998 eligibility determination, Sealaska Heritage Foundation (now Institute), the non-profit arm of the Sealaska regional Native corporation, acting on behalf of the Áak'w K̲wáan, initiated the process of nominating the site for inclusion in the National Register. In 2002 the nomination form and supporting material were formally submitted to the Alaska State Historic Preservation Office (SHPO). Between 2002 and 2005 the SHPO requested more information from Sealaska Heritage Institute concerning the boundaries and integrity of the site. Sealaska Heritage responded to these requests with additional documentation, which was accepted by the SHPO. Then, suddenly, in 2006, the SHPO asserted that TCP form had "changed so much" that it was necessary for the Alaska Historical Commission to re-review the nomination of Auke Cape. More pictures, clearer demarcation of boundaries, and additional data in support of criterion D (that "the property has yielded, or is likely to yield information important in prehistory or history") were needed. Again, Sealaska Heritage Institute, through staff anthropologist Kathy Miller, obliged this request. Significantly, the state has submitted the nomination materials to the National Register in Washington, D.C., for an informal review, and the Register office has found the documentation sufficient to go forward. Yet, as of this writing, Auke Cape is still awaiting approval as the state of Alaska's first historic site recognized under the TCP nomination process.

Is the state stalling? There does seem to be a concern among government officials, particularly at the state level, that granting TCP status to Auke Cape could open up the "floodgates" to innumerable other TCP claims and nominations, which, in turn, could "lock up" significant amounts of land to development (always a concern in Alaska, which boasts more acreage in parks and preserves than any other state, by far). However, as Bulletin 38 makes clear, TCP status itself does not preclude development; rather it requires that in federal or federally assisted undertakings, the federal agency must take into account the effect of the undertaking on the historic property, in association with the SHPO, and in consultation with people and groups for which the site has cultural and religious significance. Certainly another brake slowing the process is the fact that TCP nomination procedures are themselves still fairly new, and necessarily involve a cross-cultural grasp of landscapes, if not of models of valuing and maintaining ties to property. Thirdly, in a major Alaska city such as Juneau, where Natives are a minority (less than 20% of the population) who until recently have been cowed by racial discrimination and strict acculturation policies into practicing their culture almost invisibly, the contemporary assertion of strong cultural ties to property strikes some as surprising, at best, and a strategic "(re)invention of tradition" at worst; therefore, there is a need to proceed with caution. As the Auke Cape investigation clearly shows, however, the Tlingit claims are not merely an act of strategic essentialism (Sheridan 2005). As much as any other North American Indian group, Tlingits have maintained strong ties to historical properties through both material and symbolic means, despite discrimination and acculturation. And their record of defending properties from encroachment and dispossession, including Auke Cape, spans hundreds of years (Thornton 1997).

At base, the irresolution of the Auke Cape TCP nomination reveals some critical problems with the TCP evaluation process as it stands today. The most important of these is the political ecology of cultural models problem. Even while the TCP evaluation process itself, especially when carried out by investigators sensitive to diverse models of cultural property, becomes increasingly inclusive of cultural landscapes not previously protected under the NHPA, the state historic preservation offices and historical commissions ultimately evaluating these properties often do not include anthropologists or minorities in significant numbers. Thus, there is no way to ensure that these officials will be inclusive, and no guarantee that they will not continue to measure cultural properties against their own (or their largest constituency's) dominant cultural models, professional standards, and prototypes of what such sites consist of, rather than the TCP criteria themselves, and find them wanting. This is the essence of the political ecology of cultural models problem. This is why the Alaska SHPO wants more *written* documentation, photographs, and clearer *boundaries* for Auke Cape. A similar set of time–space boundary issues prompted the Alaska SHPO to torpedo another Tlingit TCP nomination, the Kiks.ádi Survival March Trail, in 1997 (King 2009). In the end, it appears it will be this kind of documentation, and not the story of Yeeskanaalx̱, that will secure Auke Cape's entry into the National Register. Similarly, it will be this kind of documentation that leads to successful management of Auke Cape as a TCP, not merely a "cultural park with long houses, [a] few totem poles, etc.," as has been suggested by the Juneau Parks and Recreation Advisory Committee (2005).

Conclusion: TCPs and biocultural diversity

How do you solve the political ecology of cultural models problem that hampers the successful nomination of TCPs such as Auke Cape into the National Register? Further, can the TCP process succeed in legitimizing Native American and other non-mainstream models of cultural property against the dominant cultural models that have shaped historic preservation in the United States? Clearly, it will not be easy. To begin with, it is important to note that for Native Americans the TCP model of landscape preservation is only the latest in a series of efforts to conserve their important historical sites, the vast majority of which have not succeeded. The most spectacular failure, of course, was the 1978 Native American Religious Freedom Act which was rendered virtually impotent by the Supreme Court in its 1987 *Lyng v. Indian Cemetery Protective Association* decision (United States GPO 1991; Hutt 2009). The court found that construction of a major logging road and clearcut logging operation on national forest lands, held sacred by the Yurok and Karuk Indians of northern California, did not constitute a violation of the Indians' religious freedom. Justice Sandra Day O'Connor, writing for the 5–3 majority, argued that construction of the road did not expressly prohibit the practice of the religion because the Forest Service was not proposing to prevent Indian access to their sacred sites. She failed to grasp that the logging development would have degraded the sites, and, unlike churches, these sacred landscapes could not be moved or rebuilt elsewhere. While the justices might have been sympathetic to the Indian case, overall they were bound by the dominant cultural models of both property rights and of religious practices, which in Euroamerican culture typically are tied to structures (churches) rather than geographic places. Ironically, completion of the logging road (known as the Gasquet–Orleans, or G–O, road) was prevented by environmentalists for biological (not cultural) conservation reasons, and the area was declared a "wilderness," a cultural model of landscape alien to northern California Indians.

These failures have led to more pointed efforts to protect Indian sacred landscapes, including the TCP process and President Bill Clinton's 1994 Executive Order 13007. The latter specifically directs federal land managers to "(1) accommodate access to and ceremonial use of Indian sacred sites by Indian religious practitioners and (2) avoid adversely affecting the physical integrity of such sacred sites." Neither of these processes has been tested in the Supreme Court, but if they were challenged, they would very likely face similar biases to those that crippled the American Indian Religious Freedom Act. The political ecology of cultural models of cultural property likely will not shift very much under the present Supreme Court, without legislative changes.

A better approach might be to begin a broad campaign to educate contemporary land managers and environmentalists about the virtues of recognizing Native American TCPs in particular as part of a large-scale plan to maintain not just *biological diversity*, but biocultural diversity. It goes without saying that a TCP, by virtue of having traditional cultural value in the eyes of a distinct community, may be central to maintaining diverse cultural traditions and resource bases. Furthermore, it has been shown that there is a strong correlation between Indigenous linguistic, cultural, and biological diversity in many parts of the world (Maffi 2005). To the extent that TCPs, like Auke Cape, represent diverse Indigenous cultural landscapes, they can become a tool in the effort to maintain a healthy level of biocultural diversity on the land, and to expand the narrow political–ecological framework that still governs cultural property and resource evaluations in United States. Auke Cape and Áak'w K̲wáan need each other to thrive in the future, just as they have in the past. Hopefully, the National Register nomination process will recognize this fact and act accordingly to make Auke Cape Alaska's first official traditional cultural property.

[*Guest editor's note:* In early March 2009, a representative of the SHPO informed the author that the nomination was recently approved by the state review board and will be forwarded to the National Register at an unspecified date in the future.]

Epilogue

More than 20 years after the initial Traditional Cultural Property evaluation for X'unáx̲i, Auke Cape, I am still drawn to this place. Since returning to University of Alaska Southeast in 2018, I have made a point of taking students from humanities, social science, and environmental science classes to experience this unique cultural landscape, which lies just a couple of miles from campus. I like to preface the visit with a short presentation on cultural models and perception. In the presentation I focus on two texts: 1) Nobel prize-winning novelist John Steinbeck's sensuous description of the Monterey, California, waterfront landscape which opens *Cannery Row*; and 2) L'eeneidí elder Philip Joseph's recording of the oral history of the Tlingit settling of X'unáx̲i and Áak'w K̲wáan centuries before the arrival of Joe Juneau.

John Steinbeck's passage is an overture and invitation to a story about how environmental perception lies in the eyes (and ears and nose and mindset) of the beholder, and depends on their perspective ("peephole") and relations with the constituents of that environment. It begins with a multi-sensory, multi-layered portrait of the landscape.

> Cannery Row in Monterey in California is a poem, a
> stink, a grating noise, a quality of light, a tone, a habit,
> a nostalgia, a dream. Cannery Row is the gathered and
> scattered, tin and iron and rust and splintered wood,
> chipped pavement and weedy lots and junk heaps,
> sardine canneries of corrugated iron, honky tonks,
> restaurants and whore houses, and little crowded
> groceries, and laboratories and flophouses.

Then Steinbeck moves on to describing its human inhabitants, which is not so straightforward. This is because, whether you view the inhabitants as sinners or saints varies according to your point of view, what Steinbeck calls "the peephole" you "looked through" in observing human relations in this dynamic landscape at a certain time. As a potent swirl of material, cognitive, and behavioral inputs, embodiments, flows, histories, and niche inhabitants, Steinbeck's Cannery Row is a powerful metaphor and map for understanding the dynamic cultural-ecological system that characterizes this unique Pacific coastal environment in the mid-twentieth century (although, significantly, it lacks reference to its aboriginal inhabitants).

Phillip Joseph's (1967) oral history is equally powerful, not as an overture but as a culmination and genesis—the culmination of the migration of his people to a new land at Auke Bay and the birth of Áak'w K̲wáan. How did his people decide where to settle as they navigated north in what we now know as the Little Ice Age (c. 1300-1800)? It was a decision based on intimate knowledge of coastal river valley and bay systems, and a shared cultural model of what makes a good Tlingit homeland.

> They came by Outer Point and came to Auk Bay. ..
> They landed in Fairhaven [Indian Cove, or X'unáx̲i]
> and started building. They put up big houses, huts,
> and smokehouses [and later a fort, Áak'w Noow,
> nearby]. At the same time most of the people explored
> the whole bay. They soon find Auk Lake. And they

find out the creek [G̲aat Héeni] [that] runs from the
lake is a good sockeye creek. They also found out the
herring spawns in the spring. There were all kinds of
berries, game, and shellfish food. The name "Auquwon"
[Áak'w K̲wáan] comes from the lake. In Thlinget,
lake means "auk" [áak'w] and "quwon" [k̲wáan] means
the people [dwelling there]. That's how the people
who go there were named Aukquwon. The name of
Auk Bay in Tlingit is "Auk-ta" [Áak'w Ta]. . . They
saw ducks of all kinds, many animals like bears and
mountain goats. This place suited them and they
went right back to report to the Chief. He came and
looked the place over. He told his people they will
make their settlement in Auk Village to live in winter
time. ..They built their Dipper House [of the L'eeneidí
clan] at Fairhaven. They worked for years, then they
moved to Auk Village. Why the chief took pains to
find a village site was that they needed a sandy beach
because they use canoes and also had to have a shelter
like a boat harbor . . . After the Dipper House was
moved to [downtown] Juneau it has been rebuilt four
times. So the Auk Village should be [at least] four
hundred years old.

Phillip Joseph's ancestors' perspective shows Auke Bay and the
village site at Auke Cape (Fairhaven) to be a model Tlingit homeland
of wealth and affordance, with its protected bay, exceptional spawning
herring populations, coveted sockeye and other salmon streams, rich
clam beds, productive berry patches, wetlands, and upland hunting
grounds. It is a place of possibility for security and wellbeing. And so
they made their home there, took care of the place, began to thrive and
to define Áak'w K̲wáan as a cultural landscape. This co-evolutionary
process continued until colonization came and ultimately displaced
them—or almost—such that the Tlingit cultural landscape of X'uná̲xi

became invisible to most Juneau residents, who came to view it through other cultural lenses or "peepholes."

The national recognition and historic preservation of Auke Cape as a traditional cultural property insures that this sacred site of Áak'w Ḵwáan history will never be forgotten. Still, X'unáx̱i needs to be experienced for its values to be fully grasped and appreciated. Its land and waters also need to be cared for. Its water quality needs to be improved, its herring spawning habitats and populations restored, its shellfish beds, upland forests, and grave sites tended. That's why we take students to Auke Cape—so they can comprehend not only how Áak'w Ḵwáan came to be, but what it is now, and what it might become through appreciation, respect, and nurturing of its Indigenous cultural landscape values. I hope that the University of Alaska Southeast, as an Áak'w Ḵwáan based institution of higher education and training, can continue to play a supportive role, alongside the property's owners and descendants, in the stewardship and sustainment of Auke Cape and its environs as a living, thriving cultural landscape and social-ecological system of national significance.

—*January 25, 2022*

Dr. Thomas Thornton, currently Director of Alaska Coastal Rainforest Center and Professor of Environment and Society at the University of Alaska Southeast, has carried out human ecological studies in Alaska and elsewhere for more than 30 years. His book, *Haa Léelk'w Hás Aaní Saax'u: Our Grandparents' Names on the Land*, which was published by Sealaska Heritage Institute with the University of Washington Press, won a 2012 Alaska Historical Association award.

References

Dauenhauer, Nora and Richard, editors. 1987. *Haa Shuká, Our Ancestors: Tlingit Oral Narratives*. Seattle and Juneau: University of Washington Press and Sealaska Heritage Foundation.

De Laguna, Frederica. 1972. *Under Mount Saint Elias: The History and Culture of the Yakutat Tlingít*. Smithsonian Contributions to Anthropology, vol. 7. Washington, D.C.: Smithsonian Institution Press.

DeWitt, Forrest. 1985. Tape Recordings on Juneau History. (Interview in Tlingit summarized by Nora Dauenhauer in 1997.)

Holland, Dorothy, and Naomi Quinn. 1987. *Cultural Models in Language and Thought*. Cambridge, U.K.: Cambridge University Press.

Hutt, Sherry. 2009. "The Evolution of Federal Agency Authority to Manage Native American Cultural Sites." *The George Wright Forum* 26:1:45-56.

Joseph, Phillip. 1967. "The History of the Aukquwon." *New Alaskan*, December.

Juneau Parks and Recreation Advisory Committee. 2005. Minutes of the Parks and Recreation Advisory Committee, Thursday, October 6. Online at www.juneau.org/ parkrec/documents/octoberminutes. pdf (accessed August 15, 2008).

King, Thomas F. 2009. "Rethinking Traditional Cultural Properties?" *The George Wright Forum* 26:1:28-36.

Kunz, Cecilia. 1997. "The Story of How Yees Ga Naalx Got His Name." *Juneau Empire*, April 21, 1997.

Maffi, Luisa. 2005. "Linguistic, Cultural, and Biological Diversity." *Annual Review of Anthropology* 29, 599–617.

Mobley, Charles M. 1996. "Cultural Resource Investigations at Auke Bay, Juneau, Alaska, for National Marine Fisheries Service, National Oceanic and Atmospheric Administration." Charles Mobley & Associates, Anchorage, Alaska.

NOAA [National Oceanic and Atmospheric Administration]. 1998. *NOAA/NMFS Juneau Consolidated Facility Final Environmental Impact Statement.* Washington, D.C.: National Oceanic and Atmospheric Administration, US Department of Commerce.

Parker, Patricia L., and Thomas F. King. 1990. "Guidelines for Evaluating and Documenting Traditional Cultural Properties." *National Register Bulletin 38.* Washington, D.C.: National Park Service.

Sealaska Corporation. 1975. *Native Cemetery & Historic Sites of Southeast Alaska, Preliminary Report.* Juneau, Alaska: Sealaska Corporation.

Sheridan, Thomas. 2005. "Strategic Essentialism and the Future of Ethnohistory in North America." *Reviews in Anthropology* 34:1, 63–78.

Shore, Bradd. 1998. *Culture in Mind: Cognition, Culture, and the Problem of Meaning.* Oxford: Oxford University Press.

Steinbeck, John. 1945. *Cannery Row.* Viking Press.

Swanton, John R. 1909. "Tlingit Myths and Texts." *Bureau of American Ethnology Bulletin 39.* Washington, D.C.: Smithsonian Institution Press.

Thornton, Thomas F. 2008. *Being and Place Among the Tlingit.* Seattle: University of Washington Press.

Thornton, Thomas F. 1997. "Traditional Cultural Property Investigation for Auke Cape, Alaska." Project No: 601.00, Contract No. 50ABNA600056, Livingstone Slone, Inc. Unpublished report in author's possession.

United States GPO [Government Printing Office]. 1991. Supreme Court Proceedings: 485 US 439 (1987). *Lyng vs. Northwest Indian Cemetery Protective Association.*

Visaya, Bessie. 1972. The Story of Yees-cah-halg. Letter to the Juneau City and Borough Administrative Office, October, 30, 1972.

Acknowledgments

I would like to thank Kathy Miller, Chuck Smythe, and Rosita
Worl for their input and constructive comments on this essay. Also,
I acknowledge all the many Áak'w K̲wáan and other Tlingits who
contributed to the study, especially Rosa Miller, Cecilia Kunz, Nora
Dauenhauer, Marion Ezrre, Ernie Hillman, George Jim, Charlie
Johnson, David Katzeek, Robert Loescher, Harold Martin, Herbert
Mercer, Florence Sheakley, Walter Soboleff, Amos Wallace, and Rosita
Worl.

The Long Journey from a Cultural Landscape to a Traditional Cultural Property: The Story of X'unáxi

Charles W. Smythe, Ph.D.

X'unáxi (Indian Point or Auke Cape), located in Auke Bay, Alaska, has long been the focus of political action to protect the cape from the intrusions of modern development. Because of these efforts by the Tlingit Áak'w people and the larger Juneau Indian community, the property retains most of its environmental and physical integrity. The social history of these protests constitutes an important expression of the ongoing traditional cultural and historical significance of the place to the local Indian community dating back more than 50 years. The efforts to protect and preserve Indian Point as an Indigenous landscape began in 1959, when the Áak'w wrote letters objecting to the acquisition of land by the National Park Service (NPS), which had been the location of their traditional herring fishery since time immemorial; continued in 1969 when the Juneau Native community objected to a proposal by the local municipality to subdivide a large portion of the area (Lots 3 and 4) and sell the land as residential lots; and re-occurred in the 1990s in response to a federal plan to construct a marine laboratory there (Lot 2) (see Worl and Thornton in this volume). The record of their actions serves to document the integrity of "relationship" and "condition" of Indian Point as a traditional cultural property (TCP) to the local Tlingit community, who for over 50 years repeatedly engaged in civil action to maintain their sociocultural practices and connections to the place and to protect the site from adverse effects of development.

In 1996, the National Oceanic and Atmospheric Administration (NOAA) selected X'unáx̲i as its preferred site for constructing a new consolidated office and research laboratory facility in Juneau. During consultations with Indian tribes and organizations and others, the Juneau Native community expressed strong opposition to the project as the place was sacred with documented burials and had ongoing use for making prayers and offerings to deceased ancestors, as well as its numerous important traditional historical associations with the Áak'w people going back to their first settlement in this area. Any such development would adversely and irreversibly affect the sacred, cultural, and historical integrity of the peninsula, which they regarded as a significant sacred and historic property associated with the Áak'w K̲wáan and the L'eeneidí clan in particular. The Native community requested that a study of the historical and ongoing cultural and religious significance of the place be conducted.

As part of its responsibilities under the National Historic Preservation Act, Section 10, the identification and documentation of historic properties, NOAA contracted with an independent investigator, Dr. Thomas Thornton, to determine whether all or parts of the cape constituted a traditional cultural property with ongoing *traditional cultural significance* to the Juneau Native community and therefore eligible for nomination to the National Register of Historic Places following the guidelines in National Register Bulletin 38. The 1997 report concluded that X'unáx̲i is associated with the cultural practices and beliefs of the Juneau Native community that are deeply rooted in the community's history and are important in maintaining its continuing cultural identity. In January of 1998, based on the results of Thornton's study, NOAA determined that Indian Point was eligible for listing in the National Register—the first step in listing an historic property. The Alaska State Historic Preservation Office (SHPO) concurred with this finding.

NOAA eventually constructed its facility in Lena Cove, and Sealaska Heritage Institute (SHI) continued the effort to list the property in the National Register in association with the L'eeneidí clan

Figure 1 Rosa Miller (center), Fran Houston (left), and Angie Hunt at Auke Recreation Area, April 1997, preparing to sing a traditional song to the spirits of the land. Indian Point is visible in the background. Photo courtesy of Thomas F. Thornton.

leader, Rosa Miller. This paper describes that journey, which extended for nearly 20 years after the completion of Thornton's report. As this was the first time that a TCP was nominated from Alaska, neither the Alaska staff of the NPS nor the SHPO were familiar with the process. In addition, it became apparent that the burden of preparing the necessary documentation fell on SHI as a private party. SHI was required to interact with multiple state and federal agencies that were responsible for carrying out the complicated review and approval process with which they were unfamiliar, resulting in numerous delays and postponements along the way that were not anticipated.

Registration Form

The key to nominating an historic property to the National Register of Historic Places is preparing a successful application known as the registration form and submitting it through the proper pathway to the Keeper of the National Register in Washington, D.C. This form presents all of the relevant information about the historical significance of the place and explains how it meets a number of criteria that would qualify it for listing in the National Register. The form must be reviewed and approved by several parties including the SHPO, the local municipality (in this case the City and Borough of Juneau, or CBJ), and owners of any property within the external boundary of the place. If a federal agency is a landowner in the proposed TCP, as was the case with X'unáxi, the registration form must be submitted to the Keeper by the federal agency. In the end, the nomination form must be reviewed and approved by the Keeper.

In 1999, Dr. Thornton submitted a draft registration form to SHI, identifying X'unáxi or Indian Point as a traditional cultural property. In 2001, SHI and the L'eeneidí clan leader, Rosa Miller, sent a letter to the Anchorage NPS office nominating X'unáxi as a traditional cultural property. Months later, SHI was notified that the letter should have ended up in the hands of the Designated Federal Officer of the NPS in Anchorage, but it was not forwarded to the correct office. Responding to a letter from SHI asking about the status of the nomination, NPS informed SHI that it needed to submit the nomination to the SHPO for its review and approval.

In 2002, SHI submitted a nomination package to the Alaska SHPO including the registration form, map, and Thornton's report, for its review and comment. The SHPO responded with revisions to the form and a request for more information, which SHI provided in 2003. SHI worked with SHPO to verify maps, cultural and historical information, descriptions of the current condition and integrity of the site, and specific information on the boundaries of the property. SHI submitted additional photographs and a revised map in 2004.

The SHPO then submitted the revised package to the Alaska Historical Commission for review and it was approved with testimony by SHI. The CBJ's Historic Resources Advisory Committee (HRAC) also approved the nomination package in 2004. In late 2004, based on comments received, SHI submitted a revised registration form to SHPO, which then forwarded it on to the Keeper of the National Register requesting a "preliminary review" of the application.

In 2005, the National Register responded to the SHPO with written comments on the registration form. Review comments were also received from HRAC. SHI, with assistance from HRAC and the Tongass National Forest, provided the additional information requested by the Keeper and submitted a revised nomination to the SHPO. SHPO promised a new and revised nomination by the end of July. Beginning in late 2005 and continuing for each of the next five years, SHI wrote the SHPO requesting information on the status of the nomination, which remained stalled. In 2009, the SHPO informed Dr. Thornton that the Indian Point nomination was in their backlog file for forwarding to the National Register. In late 2009, the CBJ wrote a letter of support for the nomination to the SHPO, which was endorsed by the CBJ Assembly and the HRAC.

As noted above, in situations in which a federal agency is a major landowner in a proposed National Register nomination, the federal agency is responsible for submitting the registration forms for review by the Keeper of the National Register. With this in mind, the SHPO referred the nomination to the Glacier Bay National Park and Preserve in 2010 because the park owned a large parcel on Indian Point. Unbeknownst to SHI, the park proceeded to submit the most recent registration form prepared by SHI to the NPS Federal Preservation Officer (FPO) in Washington, D.C., who responded with detailed review comments in October of that year. By this time, it seems that the SHPO had largely withdrawn from the process without informing SHI. Since the Alaska Historical Commission had approved the nomination, the SHPO apparently adopted the position that if the nomination was accepted by the Keeper then it would be acceptable by the SHPO. At SHI, which was not in this loop, uncertainty about the status of the nomination was paramount, and it was not until July of 2011 that, in response to another letter inquiring about the status of the nomination, the SHPO informed SHI of these events. In the letter, the SHPO referred SHI to Glacier Bay National Park and Preserve and extended an offer of assistance if needed. Seemingly, the way was cleared to move forward with the nomination.

Regarding the 2010 review comments on the registration form, the NPS FPO conveyed that the revised nomination did not fully address the extensive comments first provided by National Register staff in 2004 (the previous submission). The memo also advised that in the interim the registration form had been updated and the nomination must be re-submitted using the new form. Enclosed with the letter were copies of recent eligibility determinations for two Native American TCPs on the East Coast (Turners Falls and Nantucket Sound). These examples of recent National Register determinations depended heavily on traditional cultural information provided by the associated Native American tribes. When SHI received these comments from Glacier Bay National Park and Preserve in 2011, it was affirmed that SHI would lead the effort to prepare a revised nomination form, with welcome assistance from the park.

Preparation and Submission of New Registration Form

I returned to SHI in 2013 and soon thereafter turned my attention to this project. I had worked since 2001 for the NPS in the Northeast region, had written a Determination of Eligibility for a property within a national seashore and was an advisor to the National Register staff on recent eligibility determinations including Nantucket Sound (see Ruppert and Smythe 2017), so I was very familiar with the National Register process and staff. I viewed this effort as similar to making a case for a claim for a cultural item under the Native American Graves Protection and Repatriation Act, which requires strict adherence to the process, procedures, and requirements identified through regulations. In this case, it was the registration form that required attention, with clear direction provided in the extensive review comments compiled by National Register staff and to comply with the additional requirements of the new form. The remainder of this paper will discuss some key areas of revision and expansion.

Drawing the Boundary of the TCP

Tom Thornton's investigation of Indian Point as a TCP (1997) was invaluable to this effort as it carefully described the salient historical and cultural elements of significance that are represented at Indian Point and provided a major guide to the important sources of information, published and unpublished, that contributed to the nomination. He described the concept of a "shamanic landscape" of which Indian Point is an exemplar. Indian Point is associated with Native graves including shamans' graves. A shamanic landscape may be defined as any area where a shamanic spirit is believed to be active. Tlingits believed that shamans' spirits remain active in the immediate environs around the grave site. These beliefs persist even after the bodies have decomposed and human remains are no longer present. These beliefs and practices continue to shape Tlingit behavior when visiting Indian Point. The imperative is to show respect and avoid or otherwise maintain a safe distance from the places that might hold shamanic burials. Members of the Tlingit community in Juneau report that they show respect for the burials by leaving offerings in the vicinity, visiting the area for the purpose of making prayers in memory of or communicating with deceased family members, and generally treating the area with special respect due to the recognition of shamans' burials. These beliefs and practices reported by members of the Native community support the finding that Indian Point has ongoing significance as a spiritual place for the Tlingit.

One of the requirements for describing an historic property is to draw a boundary around the site. I used sections of US Geological Survey quadrangle maps to prepare an accurate base map with such boundaries drawn on it. But in keeping with the cultural construct of a shamanic landscape, the boundary drawn around Indian Point extends beyond the shoreline, so that a portion of the ocean is included. Two adjacent islands were also included within the boundary, at least one of which was reported to be associated with a burial. The cultural significance of the islands and their relation to the historic property at Indian Point was a specific question posed in review comments, which was addressed in the accompanying narrative but also illustrated in the maps. In prior years, water bodies were often found to be ineligible for inclusion in nominations by the Keeper due to the indeterminability and changeability of boundaries on water, but this perspective has changed in recent years as more non-Euro-American sites were considered for inclusion. The nomination of Indian Point was the beneficiary of such developments. The mapped position of the external boundary around Indian Point beyond the shoreline is a recognition of the shamanic element in the landscape and is not intended to be precisely measurable in feet and inches.

Adding Criterion C to the Initial Nomination

In further recognition of the importance of this place and in defining a boundary in relation to nearby locations, SHI included in its expanded nomination a claim that Indian Point is significant under criterion C, the property represents "a significant and distinguishable entity," with this description:

> X'unáxi (Auke Cape/Indian Point) represents a
> significant and distinguishable entity integral to
> Tlingit folklife traditions, cultural practices, historical
> narratives, clan identity, religion, cosmology, material
> culture, subsistence lifeways, foodways, clan *at.óowu*
> (heritage property), and social history. Auke Cape was
> the original home of the Áak'w Tlingit people when
> they first migrated to the Juneau area at least 500
> years ago. Its high cliffs served the Áak'w people as a

secure lookout site and gathering place, providing a sheltered and protected vantage point for observing the approach of visitors. The Cape is associated with a major event in Áak'w history, which raised the status of the Ĺeeneidí (Dog Salmon) clan relative to other clans through their interaction with a clan from a distant community. This event is associated with a named clan ancestor (clan leader) and is further signified by important items of intangible clan heritage property including a chiefly name or title and a song (in addition to the historical narrative which is also *at.óowu*), all of which serve to document the geographical location of this occurrence on Auke Cape. This event is thus an important component of the clan's identity. Shamans' graves are believed to be located within the external boundary of the property, which is regarded by Tlingit people as a shamanic landscape. Shamans' burials are associated with persistent cultural beliefs and practices requiring respectful interaction with spiritual forces that are believed to remain associated with shamans' graves, and such observances are an important component of contemporary spiritual practices that occur on Auke Cape. The property was a source of many food items for the Áak'w people, but it is most well-known for its herring spawning areas. Herring roe is a highly valued and culturally preferred food used in trade and ceremonial contexts. Auke Cape was a uniquely productive source of herring roe, fish and oil within the Áak'w territory. Finally, the property was the subject of repeated social action to protect and preserve its natural and environmental integrity, and its significant relationship with the Indian people of Juneau (including the Áak'w and others whose

families moved into Juneau from other communities).
As described above, the local Indian community and
organizations engaged in protests and civic actions to
protect and preserve X'unáx̱i in 1959, 1969, and in the
1990s. Indeed, this nomination is another expression
of such activity.

The addition of criterion C to the initial nomination was approved by
the SHPO, which notified GBNPP in late 2014.

Criterion B Issue

One of the reviewers from the CBJ HRAC was concerned whether
criterion B, association with "the lives of persons significant in our
past," applied to "a person known through stories." This question
relates to whether an oral tradition can be accepted as history on
which a determination may be made. SHI's submission included an
oral account of a key event that occurred on Indian Point at the site
which, according to oral history, was the first settlement established in
this region by the Áak'w K̲wáan. The narrative described an encounter
between the Áak'w K̲wáan and a Yakutat clan during which the
Áak'w leader got the better of the Yakutat visitors. This event was
memorialized in a personal name that the leader adopted, as well as a
song that was recorded by an anthropologist in the early 20th century,
confirming the Áak'w leader's authority over the land and marking
an increase in status for himself and the Áak'w K̲wáan. The SHPO
transmitted this question to the Keeper as it sought guidance on this
issue.

In response, the National Register staff offered this commentary:

> … Use of Criterion B in association with the historic
> figure, Yeeskanaal̲x (Newly Rich Man), is acceptable
> as long as the cultural traditions of the Native group
> provide strong evidence of his importance to the
> ongoing cultural beliefs and practices of that group. In

particular, the evidence appears to show a very specific connection between this site and the particular activities for which Yeeskanaal<u>x</u> is considered an important figure. The use of Criterion B would be much less appropriate if the link between the person and his activities were of only a more general nature (i.e. he lived in the village but his important actions occurred elsewhere.)

The use of stories and oral traditions to document a person and his important actions is acceptable under Criterion B since this would be the expected nature of the evidence for such traditional information. Citations in written literature or earlier ethnographic studies might help strengthen the case, but with regard to significance as a traditional cultural property, the appropriate sources are best defined by the traditional practices of the associated groups. It matters less if the figure was or was not an actual person, but rather that he exists in the traditional beliefs of the specific group. [National Register Bulletin 38 notes that under Criterion B "person" can be taken to refer to an individual whose tangible, human existence can be inferred on the basis of historical, ethnographic, or other research, and to persons such as gods or demigods who feature in the traditions of a group.]

Criterion D and Archaeological Evidence

The revised nomination included an expanded discussion of criterion D in response to questions posed by a National Register reviewer (archaeologist) and the CBJ HRAC (chaired by an archaeologist), both of whom requested a fuller discussion. Criterion D states

Figure 2 Canoe Run on Indian Point. The Tlingit cleared rocks from the shore to facilitate the landing of canoes on rocky beaches in the vicinity of their villages and camps. Photo by Chuck Smythe, 2014.

that the proposed historic property has or may be "likely to yield information important in prehistory or history." Several archaeological investigations on Indian Point carried out in anticipation of the proposed development of the NOAA fisheries research and science center were relevant. An exploratory archaeological excavation had exposed a midden that, in association with oral history, indicated traditional use of the site from 800 years ago through the 1970s. Other investigations documented the presence of several canoe runs on the beach in close proximity to the midden and numerous culturally modified trees, which deepened the evidence of habitation and probably the presence of a village at this location. One archaeologist pointed out that oral testimony collected by Thornton and others suggest that much of the traditional cultural activity that occurred on

Indian Point may have taken place at places other than that which has undergone intensive archaeological survey. "Further archaeological investigation at these other locations will likely yield important information about Áak'w Tlingits and their lives and reveal physical evidence to support the myriad of uses of Auk Cape as a Traditional Cultural Property provided in the oral testimonies" (Marvin 2005). In the revised nomination, SHI listed seven questions that could be addressed with additional information from excavations in support of criterion D: Auke Cape has yielded and is likely to yield additional information important in prehistory or history.

Final Submission of Registration Form

Working with park staff who assisted in ensuring that all necessary issues were addressed, I submitted a full package (60 pages) to the national park in January of 2014. This included the narrative form, historic and contemporary photos, seven maps, and correspondence including letters of support from local government and SHI. Three months later I received written comments and editorial clarifications from the park and notification that the park staff has consulted with the SHPO about the need to review this packet. The SHPO asked if the questions were answered from the previous review by National Register staff, and park staff replied they had been answered in this version and that the SHPO did not need to review it again.

A review comment by the park noted, "it would be **very useful** to include a map that has all of the locations the nomination describes labeled. For example, the nomination talks about Auk Nu (Áak'w Fort), Auke Lake, etc., but there is no map with these labeled. Because there are so many 'features' which include Auk (or Auke) it becomes quite confusing...." Following up on this comment, SHI prepared a map (Áak'w Kwáan Cultural Landscape, see Figure 3) of the greater Auke Bay area with 14 features identified.

I submitted a revised nomination form in May 2014 which was sent by GBNPP to the SHPO for review. SHI requested information from the park on the status of the nomination in November. In

54

Áak'w Ḵwáan Cultural Landscape, Juneau, Alaska

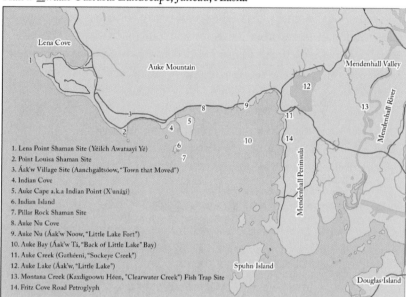

Lena Cove

Auke Mountain

Mendenhall Valley

Mendenhall River

Mendenhall Peninsula

Spuhn Island

Douglas Island

1. Lena Point Shaman Site (Yéilch Awataayí Yé)
2. Point Louisa Shaman Site
3. Áak'w Village Site (Aanchgaltsóow, "Town that Moved")
4. Indian Cove
5. Auke Cape a.k.a Indian Point (X'unáx̱i)
6. Indian Island
7. Pillar Rock Shaman Site
8. Auke Nu Cove
9. Auke Nu (Áak'w Noow, "Little Lake Fort")
10. Auke Bay (Áak'w Tá, "Back of Little Lake" Bay)
11. Auke Creek (Gathéeni, "Sockeye Creek")
12. Auke Lake (Áak'w, "Little Lake")
13. Montana Creek (Kaxdigoowu Héen, "Clearwater Creek") Fish Trap Site
14. Fritz Cove Road Petroglyph

Figure 3 Places of historic and cultural Significance to the Áak'w Ḵwáan in the vicinity of X'unáx̱i (Indian Point/Auke Cape).

December, the SHPO notified the park superintendent that the comments from the Keeper on the initial nomination had been addressed and formally concurred with the addition of criterion C. The park then requested a re-submittal by SHI to correct technical issues with the submittal (pagination on the form and labeling on the accompanying CDs) and to add a letter to the packet, which SHI completed in August 2015. The full package was then submitted by the park to the FPO in Washington, D.C.

In early 2016, the NPS historian in Anchorage realized that the Bureau of Land Management (BLM), as a land owner on Indian Point, had not been invited to comment back in 2004 when the original nomination was put forward. The BLM suggested consultations be held with the Douglas Indian Association (the federally recognized tribe based across Gastineau Channel from Juneau in Douglas that claims an interest in Indian Point) and the Central Council of Tlingit and Haida Indians of Alaska (another federally recognized tribe headquartered in Juneau). Letters of support were received from the two tribes in 2016, followed by a statement of support from the BLM. The BLM stated, "The well documented support for this nomination from the Douglas Indian Association, the Central Council of Tlingit and Haida Indians of Alaska as well as the Sealaska Corporation was significant in BLM's consideration."

With these letters attached, the packet was given to the National Register program in early May. After a 45-day public comment period, the director of the NPS announced that X'unáxi was listed on the National Register of Historic Places on July 7, 2016, nearly 20 years after it was determined eligible.

Charles W. Smythe, Ph.D., is Senior Ethnologist and the former Director of the Culture and History Dept. at Sealaska Heritage Institute. He was a Senior Anthropologist for the National Park Service and an Anthropologist for the Smithsonian Institution.

References

Marvin, Susan H. 2005. Comments on Indian Point National Register Nomination. Email from Susan Marvin, Chair of the City and Borough of Juneau's Historic Resources Advisory Committee, to Jo Antonson, Kathy Miller, and Rosita Worl, dated May 5, 2005. (Copy on file at Sealaska Heritage Institute).

Ruppert, David E., and Charles W. Smythe. 2017. "National Park Service Approaches to Connecting Indigenous Cultural and Spiritual Values to Protected Places." In Indigeneity and the Sacred: Indigenous Revival and the Conservation of Sacred Natural Sites in the Americas, Ed. by Fausto Sarmiento and Sarah Hitchner. New York: Berghahn Books.

Thornton, Thomas F. 1997. "Traditional Cultural Property Investigation for Auke Cape, Alaska." Contract Report to Livingston Slone, Inc., Anchorage, Alaska for National Oceanic and Atmospheric Administration.

Made in the USA
Middletown, DE
10 December 2022